Cornerstones of Freedom

The Story of
THE
LEWIS AND CLARK
EXPEDITION

By R. Conrad Stein

Illustrated by Lou Aronson

 CHILDRENS PRESS, CHICAGO

Library of Congress Cataloging in Publication Data

Stein, R Conrad.
    The Lewis and Clark Expedition.

    (Cornerstones of freedom)
    SUMMARY: Follows the Lewis and Clark Expedition as
it explores the sparsely populated territory between
the Mississippi River and the Pacific Ocean.
    1. Lewis and Clark Expedition—Juvenile literature.
[1. Lewis and Clark Expedition. 2. The West—
Discovery and exploration] I. Aronson, Lou.
II. Title.
F592.7.S73   917.8'04'2   78-4648
ISBN 0-516-04620-9

On the Missouri River, Captain Meriwether Lewis issued a one-word command, "Sail." The men in the long keelboat hoisted the square sail. Other men in two slender rowing boats called *pirogues* followed the keelboat. On the bank of the river a man led the group's two horses.

The Lewis and Clark Expedition, a force of more than thirty men, was beginning the most exciting mission of exploration in American history. The men had been ordered to travel through the little-known Louisiana Territory, enter the unknown Oregon country, and finally reach the Pacific Ocean.

In the early nineteenth century, knowledge of the American Northwest was so incomplete that Lewis and Clark were given what turned out to be some very strange requests.

They were asked to look for the descendants of a mysterious Welsh prince named Madoc. According to legend, Madoc and a band of followers had left the British Isles to sail to the New World some three hundred years before Columbus.

Another request came from Benjamin Rush, a famous doctor and a signer of the Declaration of Independence. Rush asked Lewis to observe the religious practices of the Western Indians. A popular belief was that those Indians were descendants of the Biblical Lost Tribe of Israel, and Rush wanted to know whether their religion resembled that of the Jews.

Even Thomas Jefferson, sponsor of the expedition and one of the most intelligent Americans in history, believed that great woolly mammoths might still roam the foothills near the Rocky Mountains.

Every member of the expedition knew that Indian country lay immediately ahead of them.

They would soon confront the Sioux warriors, the most feared tribe of the American frontier. Beyond the Sioux country was a land known only to Indians and a few hardy fur trappers. Still farther up the Missouri was a land of mystery and legend.

"I set out at 4 o'clock . . . and proceeded under a gentle breeze up the Missouri," wrote William Clark in his journal on May 14, 1804. With those words, the explorers left the frontier community of St. Louis. The Lewis and Clark Expedition plunged into the unknown.

Just a few months before the expedition left St. Louis, the United States and France had concluded the largest real estate transaction in history. At that time, Louisiana was not a state on the lower end of the Mississippi River. It was a huge territory in the middle of the present-day United States. In 1803 the United States bought the land from France for $15,000,000. Overnight, the Louisiana Purchase doubled the size of the young republic.

Little was known about the newly purchased land, and President Jefferson was eager to have it explored. To lead the expedition he chose

Meriwether Lewis, a fellow Virginian. Lewis was an energetic leader and a perfectionist who mastered every detail of a project. Jefferson and Lewis agreed that the expedition would be called the "Corps of Discovery."

Lewis was then twenty-eight years old, an army captain serving as Jefferson's personal secretary. The thought of exploring a vast, new land excited him more than anything he had ever dreamed about. He wrote his fellow army officer William Clark, asking him to share command of the expedition. The two enjoyed a perfect friendship. "I will cheerfully join you," Clark wrote back. "I do assure you that no man lives with whom I would prefer to undertake such a trip as yourself."

It is difficult to imagine how two men of such entirely different personalities maintained such a close friendship. Lewis was deeply serious about all aspects of life. He preferred being alone and was given to attacks of depression and brooding. Clark, on the other hand, was an outgoing person who liked to laugh and tell jokes. He had flaming red hair and a bright smile. The two had some things in common, however. They were both experienced woodsmen, they were superb leaders, and each of them was a crack shot with a rifle.

As they sailed up the Missouri, the river itself became an enemy. Hidden rocks and dead trees floating in the water could tear the bottom out of a boat. Early in the journey the two leaders discovered that Clark was more skilled at steering the keelboat than was Lewis. So Clark handled the rudder of the boat while Lewis, the loner, walked along the riverbank. He was usually accompanied by his pet dog, a large black Newfoundland called Scammon.

Although the river was sometimes an enemy, it also provided food for the explorers. In those days, when only a few Indian tribes hunted in the forests of the area, game was abundant near the riverbank. Hunting parties tracked game a mile or two ahead of the boats. When a deer or an elk was killed, the carcass was hung on a tree by the riverbank so the men in the boats could haul it in.

Of course, there were plenty of fish. Almost any kind of bait could be used to catch trout, bass, and catfish with ease. The men once caught a huge catfish which they guessed weighed close to one hundred pounds. They proudly showed the

fish to an Indian walking on the riverbank. The Indian nodded as if to say, "Pretty good fish." Then he said, through an expedition interpreter, "Wait till you get farther upstream. That's where the really big ones are."

As the Corps of Discovery traveled, they investigated the legends of the Louisiana Territory. Many tall tales were told about this little-known land. Not long after they left St. Louis, the two captains and ten of the men marched a considerable distance to see what the Indians called "the Mountain of the Little People." The Indians claimed that little devils only eighteen inches tall lived there. Despite the fact that they

were so tiny, they were said to be savage fighters. Only the bravest warriors would venture near this mountain. Lewis and Clark reached the mountain and climbed it. They had found nothing after an hour and finally left, even though their Indian guides kept claiming the little people would appear any minute.

The forests of Missouri soon gave way to the ocean of grass on the Great Plains. Because herds of buffalo roamed the grasslands, the party was assured plenty of food. The expedition averaged ten miles a day as it pushed upriver. If the wind were favorable the men could use their sails, but usually they had to row or pole their boats upstream.

They still had not met the Sioux Indians.

When frontier people said "Sioux" they often accompanied the word with a gesture. They drew their forefingers swiftly along their throats while saying, "Sioux!" This sign language, used by Indians, Europeans, and Americans alike, meant that the Sioux were cutthroats.

One morning in September, three Indian boys swam out to the keelboat to inform Captain Lewis that the chiefs of the Sioux nation wanted to speak with him. That same morning Sioux braves stole one of the expedition's two horses. Lewis was furious, but he remembered Jefferson's written instructions regarding the Sioux: "Of that nation we wish most particularly to make a friendly impression because of their immense power."

In the afternoon, four Sioux chiefs boarded a slim pirogue and were rowed to the keelboat. The Sioux had grown accustomed to demanding gifts from travelers along the Missouri River, but they had previously dealt only with small bands of trappers. These small groups they could bully at will. The four Sioux chiefs appeared to be a bit uneasy as they were rowed out to the keelboat. Never before had they encountered a force so large and well armed as the Corps of Discovery.

When they were on board, the Sioux first asked for tobacco and whiskey. They were given some. Meriwether Lewis looked at their faces. He felt he could deal with their main chief, a large man called Black Buffalo Bull, but he kept a wary eye on a lesser chief called The Partisan. There was something about him that Lewis did not like. Talking to the Sioux proved frustrating. They demanded gifts of rifles, powder, hunting knives, and other goods that Lewis refused to part with. Speaking through an interpreter, the words between the two men grew angry. Suddenly the lesser chief—The Partisan—collapsed on the deck. Drunkenly he crawled toward the bow. He's putting on an act, Lewis thought. The Indian had had only a sip of whiskey. He couldn't possibly be drunk.

Politely but firmly Lewis asked the four Sioux chiefs to leave the keelboat. Still muttering their demands for gifts, the chiefs got back into the pirogue. Manned by Captain Clark and four oarsmen, they were rowed to the riverbank. About one hundred angry braves were waiting there. In a whisper, Lewis ordered the men in the keelboat to load their rifles.

The pirogue bumped against the riverbank. A dozen braves rushed it. Two of them grabbed the rope tied to the bow and refused to let Clark return to the keelboat. The Partisan, still acting drunk, grabbed at Clark's clothes.

A furious William Clark drew his sword.

"Take aim," ordered Lewis from the keelboat, and more than thirty rifles suddenly pointed at the Indians on the riverbank. The Sioux, in turn, readied their bows and arrows. A moment of electric silence passed.

Finally the Sioux chief yielded. He must have known the power of the rifles and was fearful of losing half his braves. He ordered his men to release the rope of the pirogue and allow Clark to return to the keelboat. When the pirogue joined the keelboat The Partisan, now clearly sober, watched the expedition move upstream. He kicked at the dirt of the riverbank, angry that his tribe had lost the confrontation with the men of the Corps of Discovery.

Snow began to whirl on the last day of October, and chunks of ice banged against the sides of the boats. Lewis and Clark made a winter camp with a group of friendly Mandan Indians who lived near present-day Bismarck, North Dakota.

The Mandan had seen a few white men, but they were astonished by the sight of York, the only black member of the expedition. The remote Mandan had never seen a black man. Their chief refused to believe that York was really black. He thought he was a white man who for some reason painted himself black. The chief wet his finger and tried to rub off the "black paint" on York's arm. He shook his head in disbelief when his rubbing had no effect. York, a giant of a man with a gentle nature, loved the attention he received from the Mandan.

During that winter with the Mandan one of the men, Toussaint Charbonneau, was suddenly visited by his wife. Charbonneau was a French Canadian who had lived among the Indians. He was a whiskey-guzzling loafer whose only real value to the expedition was as an interpreter. While living with the Indians he had purchased

a slave girl named Sacajawea and made her one of his squaws. Sacajawea was a Shoshone Indian, native to the Rocky Mountain area. She had been only a girl when captured by Sioux Indians and sold to Charbonneau. Now she was a teenager, soon to have her first child.

Because Sacajawea could speak the Shoshone language, Lewis and Clark agreed to take her with the expedition when they left the following spring. They had no idea how valuable the presence of the young Indian girl would be in the coming months.

In April of 1805 the party again ventured up the Missouri River. They sent the keelboat downriver with letters to President Jefferson and some samples of plant and animal life found on the Great Plains. Their flotilla now consisted of the two pirogues and six small canoes. This time Sacajawea traveled with them. Carried on her back was her two-month-old baby, Baptiste, who had been born in the Mandan camp.

Before Lewis left, the Mandan told him he would soon encounter huge brown bears that attack man on sight and are impossible to kill. Lewis dismissed the story of monster bears as merely another Indian tall tale. He had yet to see a grizzly bear.

Once beyond the Mandan village, the Missouri River cut through a truly unknown world, where few Indians had ever set foot.

Tall trees sprouted up in the grassland. Deer, elk, moose, and buffalo were so abundant that Lewis wrote, "two good hunters would conveniently supply a regiment with provisions." These animals had never seen men before and had no fear of them. A buffalo calf attached himself to William Clark and followed him around like a puppy. The men saw antelope herds so huge that they supported wolf packs.

The wolves roamed about the flanks of the herds, bringing down the weak and the feeble. Even though the game was so plentiful, expedition hunters did not overkill. "Although game is very abundant and gentle," Lewis wrote, "we kill only as is necessary for food."

The Missouri River now flowed through the present-day state of Montana, and supported the finest beaver country in North America. Beaver dams sparkled under the trees on both sides of the river. Thousands of playful otters frolicked in the water. Not many years later, fur trappers would destroy this paradise.

One morning Captain Clark discovered a huge bear track in the mud by the riverbank. It was half again the size of any bear track he had ever seen. While paddling up the river later that day, the men saw in the distance two bears feeding on berries. One of them stood on his hind legs to eat from a top branch. The men thought their eyes were playing tricks on them. The bear seemed to be eight feet tall.

The next morning two expedition hunters burst into camp, running for their lives. After catching their breath they explained that they

had been chased by a monstrous bear that refused to die even though it had been shot four times. Lewis and another man set out to look for the animal. They did not have to look far. From their left they heard a roar and saw a huge, bloody grizzly bear lumbering toward them. Lewis fired and hit the animal in the chest. His companion also scored a hit. The grizzly continued his charge, ignoring the shots as if they were the stings of flies. The two men ran and the grizzly chased Lewis to the river, where the desperate captain jumped in. He stood in waist-high water and turned to face the bear. The captain drew his knife, although he knew it would be a feeble weapon against the grizzly. Probably because of his wounds, the bear did not follow Lewis into the river. Instead, it roared one last time and disappeared into the woods. After that, the members of the Corps of Discovery often found themselves looking over their shoulders, terrified of seeing another grizzly.

The once wide Missouri was now becoming a narrow stream as it cut toward the Rocky Mountains. This land was the home of Sacajawea. Although they had yet to meet her people, the Indian girl could point out to Lewis and Clark places along the riverbank where she used to pick wild onions. She kept talking of a magnificent waterfall farther upstream.

One morning Lewis hiked alone ahead of the party. He thought he heard something that sounded like distant thunder. The roaring grew louder, and he knew the sound came from falling water. He rounded a bend, and then stood in frozen astonishment. The mighty Missouri tumbled down a falls more than eighty feet high. The water pounding on the rocks below burst upward into a sheet of fine spray where rainbows danced. It was then Lewis wrote that he wished he could have been a painter, "that I might be able to give the enlightened world some just idea of this truly magnificent and sublimely grand object, which has from the commencement of time been concealed from the view of civilized man." Lewis was at Great Falls, Montana, where today a power dam has altered the spectacular view he once beheld.

In August the Corps of Discovery arrived at a plain where the Missouri divides into three rivers. They named the largest one Jefferson after their sponsor, and followed it upstream. The country was mountainous now, and at many points they were faced with roaring rapids. The men had to carry their canoes more often than they were able to ride in them.

Lewis hiked miles ahead of the party with a private named Hugh McNeal. The river became so narrow they could jump across it. Finally, they could straddle it. At that point Hugh McNeal bowed his head and offered a prayer. He thanked God for letting him live to see the day when he could behold the broad Missouri with one foot on either side of it.

Later that same day, the two discovered another stream. Lewis stopped to take a drink. He stared at the water with a puzzled expression on his face. "West," he finally said. "This stream is flowing west." It was true. Throughout their long journey the explorers had been struggling against rivers that flowed east to enter the Mississippi. Without knowing it the two men had crossed the Continental Divide. From now on the waters they would encounter would flow west to empty into the destination of the Corps of Discovery—the Pacific Ocean.

At this point, however, they were out of river country. Facing them were the towering Rocky Mountains. They would need horses to cross the mountains. Sacajawea had assured Lewis and Clark that her people would sell horses to the expedition. But where were the Shoshone? The expedition had seen traces of Indians—a lost moccasin and an old campsite. Sacajawea's people, however, were keeping to themselves. In five months of travel from the Mandan village in North Dakota to the foothills of the Rockies, the explorers had not seen a single human being.

The Shoshone were a small tribe who lived in constant fear of their powerful neighbors, the Blackfeet. They hid themselves in small villages in the mountains and were suspicious of all outsiders. One morning an expedition hunting party discovered a lone Shoshone on horseback. They made friendly gestures to him, but the Indian galloped away.

Finally they met three Shoshone women who led them to their village. There Lewis met the Shoshone chief, a tall, lean man named Cameahwait. Using sign language, Lewis explained that he needed horses and was willing to trade for them. Cameahwait debated the request with his fellow braves. An argument started. One brave insisted that Lewis was part of a plot and was working for their enemies, the Blackfeet. Lewis did manage to convince the chief to allow one of his men to find Captain Clark and the others and lead them to the Shoshone village. But it looked as if he would never be able to persuade the Indians to give up some of their horses. Lewis had the sick feeling that without horses the journey of the Corps of Discovery would end right here, at the foothills of the Rocky Mountains.

Chief Cameahwait and the others were still arguing as Captain Clark and the rest of the expedition trudged uphill. Then a miracle happened. Sacajawea suddenly dashed toward the chief, wildly calling his name. The two were soon locked in a tearful embrace. Later, Sacajawea told the astonished captains that Cameahwait was her brother, whom she had not seen in six years.

With Sacajawea to do the bargaining, the expedition was soon off again. This time they traveled on foot, with eleven Shoshone horses and a mule as pack animals.

It was late September, and snow was beginning to fly as the explorers entered the Rocky Mountains. They followed the Lolo Trail, an ancient Indian path that wove in between and over mountain peaks. Almost every morning they woke up to freezing rain or pelting snow. Footing was treacherous, and even the surefooted Shoshone horses tumbled on the winding trail. As soon as the expedition struggled up one mountain peak they discovered an even higher one directly in front of them.

A scarcity of game in the Rockies made their struggle even more desperate. Time after time, parties of their best hunters came back empty-handed. Sacajawea was an expert at digging edible roots from the soil, but roots could not sustain the men for long. They were soon eating candles. Finally, they were forced to eat several of their precious pack animals.

William Clark, leading a band of hunters, forged ahead on the trail. The men had traveled for days without seeing anything to shoot. Suddenly Clark found himself on a mountaintop looking down at an immense valley. He held his breath, hoping this valley was no illusion.

Finally he laughed out loud, knowing he had at last made it through the Rocky Mountains.

Below him was the lush green forest of the Clearwater Valley in what is now Idaho. After having struggled over one mountain ridge after another, this flat valley suddenly stretching to the horizon looked to him like the Garden of Eden.

In the Clearwater Valley the explorers built dugout canoes and started downstream. They were now in the wildly beautiful Snake River country, with green timberland on both sides of the river. Game increased and red salmon could be caught with nets.

The expedition had crossed the boundary of the United States; the men had traveled even beyond the newly purchased Louisiana Territory. They were now in the Oregon country, a land claimed by several European powers. The exploration of Lewis and Clark gave great weight to the United States' claim on Oregon.

As the Snake River flowed into the Columbia River, the group passed many Indian villages. These tribes had traded with sailors from ships in the Pacific. Lewis saw one of them wearing a black Navy pea coat.

It was pouring rain on the morning of November 7, 1805, as the party neared present-day Astoria, Oregon. After the rain, a blanket of thick fog covered the explorers in their canoes. When the fog finally cleared, they saw a sight many of them never really believed they would see. Lewis wrote, "we enjoyed the delightful prospect of the ocean—that ocean, the object of all our labors, the reward of all our anxieties." The gleaming Pacific spread before them, and they heard the roar of waves breaking on the beach. Their incredible goal had been realized.

Arrival at the Pacific was not the end of the trail. The expedition still had to return home. Originally, the two captains had hoped to find a ship heading to the eastern half of the United States by way of Cape Horn. Lewis had a letter of credit, written by President Jefferson himself, guaranteeing payment to any ship captain who would take the expedition back to civilization. Throughout the long winter, however, no ship passed the Oregon coast. Lewis and Clark decided to return the same way they had come—by canoe when possible, on foot when not.

The journey back to civilization was just as difficult, but not quite as spectacular, as the trip to the Pacific had been. When they passed the Mandan village in North Dakota, Sacajawea and her husband decided to stay. All the men would miss the small Indian girl who had done so much to make the Lewis and Clark expedition a success. They would also miss her son, Baptiste, who was now more than a year old.

Twenty-nine men and Lewis's dog Scammon sailed triumphantly into St. Louis on September 23, 1806, nearly two and one-half years after they had set sail from that same city. Through-

out the hardships they had encountered and the thousands of miles they had traveled, only one man had been lost. Sergeant Charles Floyd had died of an illness only three months after the expedition began. He was the first American soldier to be buried west of the Mississippi. The rest of the crew were the same men who had originally sailed with Lewis and Clark.

The Lewis and Clark expedition had traveled the length of the Missouri, crossed the Rocky Mountains, reached the Pacific Ocean, and come back again. Most of this incredible journey was over completely unknown land. It was an exploring achievement that will not be repeated unless one day man sets foot on some far-off planet.

About the Author

R. Conrad Stein was born and grew up in Chicago. He enlisted in the Marine Corps at the age of eighteen, and served for three years. He then attended the University of Illinois, where he received a Bachelor's Degree in history. He later studied in Mexico and earned a Master of Fine Arts degree from the University of Guanajuato. He now lives in Mexico, where he is a member of the PEN writers group of San Miguel de Allende.

The study of history is Mr. Stein's hobby. Since he finds it to be an exciting subject, he tries to bring the excitement of history to his readers. He is the author of many other books, articles, and short stories written for young people.

About the Artist

For **Louis Aronson,** painting and illustrating are both career and hobby. He teaches art at the Chicago Academy of Fine Art and has illustrated children's books, magazines, and other publications. He does large paintings for relaxation.

Mr. Aronson lives with his family in Oak Park, a Chicago suburb. When he does children's books, his two sons sometimes act as his models.

After graduating with a Bachelor's Degree in art from the University of Illinois, Mr. Aronson joined the army. He was sent to Viet Nam after attending language school. After leaving the service, he returned to school at the Art Center College of Design in California to study illustration. He has earned several awards in this field.